This book was inspired by actual
events I sincerely hope that it
serves as an example of what
kind of foundation we can set for
our children. We must be diligent
as parents to not only prepare
our children for life, but to
also teach them core values
that will never part from them.

D1608264

We can't change the wind or the sea
but we can change the sail!
I wish you peace.

To Noodah, Woodah, & Poodah daddy
loves you dearly

Arielle's father picked her up from school one day and she was visibly sad.

When she got in the car he asked. Hey babygirl what's wrong?She looked at him with a sad expression and began to cry. She said the children at this new school teased me about my hair! He replied oh no what did they say?

She explained they picked at my hair
because it stands on top of my head!
They called me names like puff puff
and bush baby. I don't like this school or
any of the people either.

Her father chuckled and smiled. He said my beautiful princess.

Don't you know your hair is a crown?

Arielle replied really daddy? Why do you say that?

He began to explain to her that hair was powerful and that many beautiful women in history had hair just like hers.

She was no longer upset and wanted to hear more. She asked daddy can you show me some of those beautiful women? He replied yes my Princess of course I can!

Once they were home Arielle's father went to the family computer and began to show her all the beautiful women he spoke of.

He showed her Cleopatra the beautiful Queen of Egypt and
Mary McLeod Bethune the great educator and civil rights leader.

Arielle learned about the great journalist and civil rights leader Ida B. Wells.

He showed her Alice Walker the great writer and Mae Jemison the first black woman in space.

He showed her Nzingha the great Amazon Queen of Matamba.

He showed her two great singers. The wonderful Lauryn Hill and the soulful Nina Simone.

He showed her Shirley Chisolm the Congresswoman and Babara Jordan the State Representative.

She learned about Toni Morrison the great novelist and Sojourner Truth the women's rights activist

Arielle felt better and she wanted to learn everything about these great women that had hair like hers. She said daddy can I do something great like these strong women?

He replied, of course you can be anything you set your mind to be!

She replied said thank you thank you daddy. I love you so much and guess what else daddy.

What's that Princess? He asked.

I really really love my crown it makes me special. Her father smiled and said that's right Princess you are very special.

That night Arielle went to bed very happy and while she slept she had a dream. She saw herself in all those great women. She saw herself singing like Lauryn Hill and going into space like Mae Jemison. She took the podium to speak like Sojourner Truth. She printed newspapers like Ida B. Wells She even prepared her warriors for battle like Queen Nzingha.

Then a very special woman with a long gown and a beautiful feather in her hair visited Arielle. She was the most beautiful of all the women. Arielle cried tears of joy and asked who she was.

The woman just told her I am you and you are me
and you can be what your heart desires to be.
The woman then smiled and said love who you are
my Princess and disappeared.

Arielle woke up excited the next day. She told her parents I don't need to leave my new school. I love myself above all else and others will love me too.

She went to school with a big smile on her face. A kid said to her look at your hair it's so puffy. She replied you mean like Queen Nzingha! The other kids asked who is that. Arielle replied a great African Queen that's who! The kid then said oh bigdeal your hair is still bushy. She said like Nina Simone. Wow who is that they asked. She said one of the greatest singers of all time. My hair is just like hers.

The kids were all amazed. They crowded around Arielle.
She began to tell them about all the beautiful women that
had hair like hers.

The kids now wanted to be friends with
her and were asking all kinds of questions.

She then explained to them I am you and you are me and you can be what your heart desires to be.

THE   END

73203356R00015

Made in the USA
Lexington, KY
07 December 2017